drugs

Bridget Lawless

Se   Editors: Steve Barlow and Steve Skidmore

Heinemann

065113

Published by Heinemann Educational Publishers
Halley Court, Jordan Hill, Oxford OX2 8EJ
A division of Reed Educational and Professional Publishing Ltd

OXFORD   MELBOURNE   AUCKLAND
JOHANNESBURG   BLANTYRE   GABORONE
IBADAN   PORTSMOUTH NH (USA)   CHICAGO

05 04 03 02 01
10 9 8 7 6 5 4 3 2 1
ISBN 0 435 21495 0

Photos: page 7 – Andy Johnstone/Impact; page 11 – Tom Wichelow/PYMCA;
page 15 – Jeremy Feldman/Camera Press; page 17 – Nils Jorgensen/Rex Features;
page 21 – Empics; page 23 – Rex Features; page 27 – Steve Parry/Impact.
Cover design by Shireen Nathoo Design
Cover artwork by Shireen Nathoo Design
Designed by Artistix, Thame, Oxon
Printed and bound in Great Britain by Biddles Ltd

Tel: 01865 888058 www.heinemann.co.uk

Contents

What are drugs?

Drugs are things that change:

- the way you feel
- how you think
- the way you see the world.

You may have heard that all drugs are bad. But some drugs are very useful.

'Drugs' can mean medicines that treat illness or take away pain. But 'drugs' also describes a wide range of other things people take just for the effects.

Taking drugs means taking risks. They can damage your body or mind for a short time – or forever. Every year, many people become ill or die from using drugs. Others become 'hooked'. Drugs take over their life.

Did you know?

Drugs can be pills, capsules, powders, liquids, plants, gases, resins and even some household products. We often call them substances, to cover all the different forms.

Which drugs are against the law?

Most drugs are controlled by law. Controlled drugs are often called 'illegal' drugs. That means having, using, making, growing or selling them is illegal.

Use or abuse?

Some medicines and household products can be used in the wrong way (abused). Then they are covered by drug laws. This includes things like glue, cigarette lighter fluid and aerosol sprays. Some people sniff them to get 'high'.

Drugs that are legal

Alcohol and tobacco are drugs that are legal in the UK. Adults can use them openly, within certain limits. But many people believe these drugs are more dangerous than some of the illegal ones.

Caffeine is a legal drug found in tea, coffee or cocoa. Caffeine is not covered by any drug laws.

Sheila, a doctor who works in London, says:

Smoking cannabis seems to help ease pain in some serious conditions. I hope one day we can legally prescribe it.

Who takes drugs?

People have taken drugs for thousands of years. Wanting to change how we feel seems to be part of human nature!

Today, people who use drugs are of every age, race, background and class. They are not all homeless, out of work or in a mess. The highest number of users are aged between 18 and 29.

Most young people who use drugs just take them now and then. No one sets out to get a 'drug habit'. But some people who try drugs do end up with a serious problem.

The club and dance scene

The drug Ecstasy is a big part of the dance scene. Many people take Ecstasy every week, because they feel it makes clubbing more exciting.

More than a third of young people say they have tried some kind of illegal drug. Cannabis is most commonly used.

Older drug users

As people get older, they often lose interest in using illegal drugs. They are more likely to drink or smoke.

Some people who try drugs when they are young carry on taking them now and then. Cannabis is the drug most likely to be used like this. Many people smoke it with friends, just as some people go for a drink at the pub.

All sorts of people regularly use illegal drugs. It has been reported that some lawyers, police officers and judges admit to using drugs, too. Many people say drugs help them unwind or cope with stress, or just keep them awake.

Many people smoke cannabis with friends, just as some people go for a drink at the pub.

Why do people take illegal drugs?

Usually, people take drugs because they like the way drugs change their mood. Drugs might make them feel clever, funny or relaxed. Or they may make the world seem more amazing. Others take drugs because they like the risks. Even the danger of getting caught may seem exciting to them.

To fit in, or escape

Some people take drugs to be part of a crowd or gang. It is something they can do together. They may be afraid that their friends will lose interest in them if they do not take drugs.

Others take drugs to escape from things that are difficult. They might not be coping with school, college, things at home, or their job. Or they may be worried, lonely or unhappy.

Drugs cannot put right things that are wrong in someone's life. They are more likely to cause problems. But for some people, drugs can be a way of blotting out bad thoughts, feelings or events.

How some people got started

Jake, 17, a
student, says:

> I started smoking cannabis when I was 15. My friends had some. It made me feel sick and dizzy at first. But I made myself try it again. Now I enjoy it when I go out at weekends, or round a friend's house.

Sarah, 19, a
sales assistant, says:

> The crowd I go clubbing with got me started on Ecstasy. Some people take a few at a time. I can only cope with one. I don't like the idea of taking drugs, but I think clubbing wouldn't be the same without them.

Lee, 19, a
printer, says:

> I took drugs just once. By mistake. Someone put LSD in my drink. I was tripping for 14 hours, scared out of my mind. I was running about in the traffic shouting at people. I ended up in hospital. I never found out who spiked my drink. It put me off drugs.

What effects do drugs have?

Drugs have four main kinds of effect on your body or mind.

Stimulant drugs wake you up or excite you. They include amphetamines (speed), cocaine, crack, caffeine and Ecstasy.

Depressants calm you down. They lower your spirits or make you feel more peaceful. Depressants include alcohol, tranquillisers and sleeping pills.

Pain killers can make you feel calm, relaxed or sleepy. They include heroin, opium and morphine.

Hallucinogens make you see, hear or imagine things that are not real. Drugs that make you hallucinate include LSD ('acid'), magic mushrooms and Ecstasy (also a stimulant).

The effect a drug has can depend on:
- the person's mood, where they are and who they are with
- whether they have eaten, or taken other drugs or alcohol.

Drugs do not only have an effect at the time they are taken. The effects can carry on.

Short-term effects

As the 'high' of a drug wears off, the effects change. The person might feel very low. This is called 'coming down'.

Some effects of a drug may still be felt over the next few days. The person may feel tired, moody, low or in a panic for no reason. It might be hard to sleep or work. They may feel much worse than if they had not taken drugs in the first place!

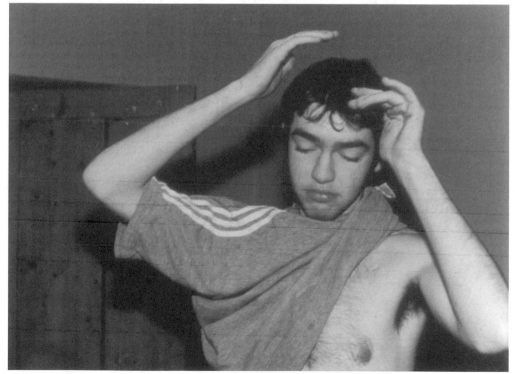

As the effects of a drug wear off, people sometimes feel tired, scared or ill.

Bad results

Drugs do not always make a person feel happy or 'high'. Sometimes the opposite happens. The person has a really bad time. They may not like the effects of the drug, but are unable to stop it. It can be very frightening.

Hidden dangers

Sometimes a drug will have a bad effect that is really dangerous. One person might take a drug and be fine. Another person can take the same drug and be very sick, pass out or even die. Everyone is different. People can also be allergic to some drugs just as other people are very allergic to certain foods.

Most of the bad effects of drugs wear off after a while. But anyone who feels any of these things after taking a drug should ask for help.

Long-term effects

Long-term effects build up when drugs are taken over months or years. Many drugs are harmful to the body if used often, or over a long period of time. The heart, lungs, liver and kidneys can all be damaged by different drugs.

It is not only illegal drugs that carry these risks. Smoking cigarettes and drinking too much alcohol also do serious damage to the body.

> Far more people die from smoking cigarettes or drinking too much alcohol than from taking illegal drugs.

Changing who you are

Drugs can change how a person thinks or behaves. They can make people feel scared all the time. They may not be able to trust anyone. They may think things are happening that are not. They may feel everyone is against them. Some drugs can make a peaceful person become violent.

How are drugs taken?

Drugs are taken in many different ways. People usually pick the way that gives the fastest, strongest effect.

Smoking

Some drugs are smoked by rolling the drug into a kind of cigarette, (called a joint, spliff or reefer). Or some of the drug can be heated in silver foil or a spoon. The smoke is sucked off through a tube. The drug quickly enters the system through the lungs.

Sniffing

Drugs in powder form may be sniffed through a straw. They enter the blood through the skin in the nose and throat.

The strong smelling gas ('vapour') from glue or sprays is usually sniffed from the can. Or glue is put in a bag or crisp packet and sniffed from that. The rush goes straight to the head. Sniffing these products is very dangerous. Some users have died because their heart or breathing stopped.

Two people die every week in the UK from sniffing solvents. Most are between 14 and 17 years old.

Injecting drugs

Drugs are often injected into the veins using a needle and syringe. Injecting adds lots of risks.

Infections

Needles and syringes that are not perfectly clean ('sterile') can cause serious infections. Dirt or germs can poison the blood, or lead to sores that will not heal.

HIV/AIDS

Many people who inject drugs get the HIV virus. Their bodies cannot fight off illness. Sharing a needle can pass the virus from one person to another. Hundreds of people die from HIV/AIDS in Britain every year.

Drugs are not the only danger. Using needles carries many risks.

Where do drugs come from?

Drugs like Ecstasy, LSD and amphetamines are man-made from chemicals. Many drugs come from plants and are grown as crops. Cannabis is mostly grown in India, Asia and North Africa. Heroin comes from opium poppies grown mostly in Asia and Turkey. Cocaine comes from the South American coca bush.

Who makes money from drug crops?

The farmers who grow these crops may not make much money. Their land is often owned by rich criminals called drug barons. They sell the drugs for a big profit. Armed guards protect the crops. The farmers have to do as they are told.

Dangerous work for the farmers

Sometimes the government of another country wants to stop illegal drugs ending up on their streets. They burn drug crops, or spray them from the air with powerful weed killers. The people, animals and food crops in the area get sprayed with these poisons too.

Drug trafficking

Transporting illegal drugs from one country to another is called trafficking. The drugs are hidden in lorries, cars, boats or planes. A lot of drugs are seized by police and Customs officers every year. But plenty still get through.

Drug couriers

Often a person called a courier is hired to carry illegal drugs into a country. They may hide the drugs in their bag or under their clothes. Sometimes they put the drugs in condoms and swallow them. If a condom bursts, they might die. X-rays can show if someone has swallowed drugs. Couriers take a big risk of being caught and punished.

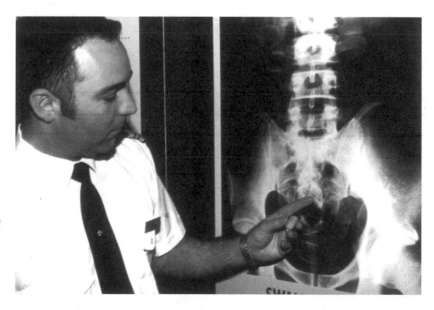

An X-ray can show drugs being carried in a courier's stomach.

Drugs and the law

If someone is caught with illegal drugs, they may be arrested. The police can do tests to see if someone has taken drugs or drunk alcohol.

Three strikes and you're out

In Britain, young people get three 'chances' for drug offences:

First offence:	A spoken warning
Second offence:	Warned and sent to the local Youth Justice Service
Third offence:	Straight to court

Adults caught with a small amount of drugs for their own use may get a spoken warning. This is called a caution. It is instead of a fine or prison. But it goes on their criminal record.

Court punishments

If someone is found guilty on a drugs charge in court, they may be released on probation. They may have to get special help with their drug problem. People can also be fined or sent to prison for drug offences. Drug dealers and traffickers face the biggest punishments. In some parts of the world, you can be beaten or put to death for drug offences.

Should drugs be legal?

Some people believe that using drugs should not be against the law. They think adults should choose for themselves. Here is what some people say about making drugs legal:

a teacher from Manchester says:

Drugs would be safer. They would be sold in measured amounts and be better quality. Health and safety warnings could be printed on the packet, like with cigarettes.

There would be less crime. Drugs would be sold in licensed shops. There would be fewer criminals involved in selling drugs. Drug gangs would stop fighting and killing each other.

a police chief from the Midlands says:

a drug advisory worker from Bristol says:

People with a drug problem could get help and advice. They would not be worried about getting in trouble with the law.

Drugs should never be made legal. People don't understand what they can do to you. It took me two months to get hooked on heroin and six years to get off it.

Damon, 25, an ex-drug addict from Glasgow says:

Drugs in the news

Drugs and the stars

Many pop stars, film stars and models admit taking drugs. They may use them for fun, or to help them deal with being famous. Sometimes they take drugs to help them stay thin.

Don't do as I do

A lot of people follow what the stars do and say. But when a famous person admits using drugs, they set a bad example to young people. Most stars only admit using drugs when they have become a problem. Then they warn other people not to do the same as them.

People in power

Men and women in positions of power and responsibility are often asked if they have taken drugs. It puts them on the spot! They do not want to lose their job or lose votes by saying the wrong thing!

Drugs and sport

The world of sport has its own problems with drugs. Many athletes use drugs called steroids to help build up their strength. Some drugs help make more muscle when you train. Some give extra power and lasting energy. These things can give the person a better chance of winning.

Cheating to win

Using drugs to help your performance is against sporting rules. It is cheating. If tests show someone has taken drugs, their career may be destroyed. Some people think it is worth the risk. After all, a successful athlete can earn lots of money. Sportswear companies pay large amounts to sponsor popular athletes.

Canadian athlete Ben Johnson lost his gold medal at the Seoul Olympics in 1988, because he took illegal drugs.

Types of drugs

Amphetamine (am-fet-a-meen)
speed, whizz, uppers, pep pills

Amphetamine is usually a white powder. It can be sniffed, swallowed or injected. It gives the user lots of energy. They can stay up all night dancing, working or studying. But afterwards, they may feel unhappy, tired and moody.

Amyl Nitrate (am-il nite-rate)
poppers, rush, liquid gold

This is a clear golden liquid, usually found in a small brown bottle. The vapours are sniffed to give a short rush. The user feels dizzy and high for a few minutes.

Cannabis
dope, blow, pot, draw, puff, hash, grass, weed

Cannabis is the most popular of the controlled drugs. It can look like dried herbs or a brown or greenish block. It is usually smoked in specially rolled cigarettes. The user feels stoned. They may be relaxed, chatty or quiet, or find everything very funny.

Cocaine
coke, Charlie, C, toot, snow

Cocaine is a white powder. It is usually sniffed, smoked, or injected. The user feels confident. Their mind works fast and clearly. Afterwards they may feel tired and down.

Crack
freebase, base, rock, stone

Crack is a white crystal lump made from cocaine. It can be smoked or injected. The user feels a big rush that quickly wears off. The need to take more makes it very addictive.

Ecstasy
E, doves, M25s

Ecstasy comes as pills or capsules. The user feels happy and loving towards other people. Ecstasy can kill if the person gets too hot or has an unusually bad reaction to it.

For many people Ecstasy = dance energy.

Heroin
smack, junk, horse

Heroin is a brown or white powder. It is used medically to relieve serious pain. When people use it illegally to get high, they inject or smoke it. It is very addictive.

LSD
acid, trips, tabs

LSD is a hallucinogenic drug. It comes as tablets or is sold as a square of paper with a drop of LSD on it. The effects ('trips') can last 12 hours. They are a wild mixture of exciting or scary feelings, ideas and images.

Magic mushrooms
liberty caps, mushies

These are tiny brown mushrooms that grow wild in fields. They can be eaten or taken as a tea. The effects are hallucinogenic, like a milder form of LSD. Many kinds of mushroom and toadstool look the same. Taking the wrong ones can kill.

Steroids
roids, gear, juice

Steroids are used illegally by body-builders and sportspeople to make more muscle. Some people take them to get high. They can make people very violent. They can also make men grow breasts and women grow beards.

Tranquillisers
tranx, eggs, jellies, downers

Tranquillisers are medicines used to make people calm, or help them sleep. They are addictive and very dangerous mixed with alcohol. They are usually swallowed or injected.

Volatile substances
solvents, glue, gas, aerosols

These are things that have a strong smelling vapour. People sniff them to get high. Some people sniff with a plastic bag over their head to hold the vapour. This is very dangerous.

Legal drugs

Alcohol

Alcohol has been used and abused more than any drug in history. Most people can enjoy a few drinks. But too much alcohol can make a person more likely to argue or pick a fight. If they keep drinking, they may be sick or pass out.

Someone who has drunk a lot may have a hangover the next day. They will have a bad headache and feel shaky and ill. Someone who is addicted to alcohol is called an alcoholic. They may find it hard to work or look after their family. They may also become violent.

Drinking and driving

Alcohol affects the way your body and mind work together. It is harder to operate machinery or drive a car safely. Drink-drivers cause thousands of road accidents every year.

Tobacco

Tobacco contains the addictive drug nicotine. Millions of people all over the world are hooked on cigarettes.

For years, tobacco companies said there was no risk in smoking. Now they admit they knew about the dangers long ago.

Smoking causes lung and throat cancer and heart disease. Thousands of smokers are claiming money from tobacco companies because smoking has damaged their health.

Non-smokers can suffer the same diseases if they share their home or office with someone who smokes. They can't help breathing the smoke in. Unborn babies are harmed if their mother smokes while pregnant.

Thirty-three thousand people die from alcohol abuse in the UK every year. Half of all long-term smokers will be killed by their habit.

Helplines and websites

Helplines

You can phone these numbers to find out more about drugs or get advice. Calls are private. No one else will be told about your call.

National Drugs Helpline: (0800) 776600
24-hour free phone line for drugs advice.

Drugs in Schools: (0808) 8000800
Free phone line 10am–6pm Monday to Friday.

Release: (0207) 7299904
Legal and drugs advice. Standard cost calls.
10am–6pm Monday to Friday.
Emergency line: (0207) 6038654
For calls outside usual hours. Standard cost.
Email: **info@release.org.uk** to ask questions or get advice.

ISDD (Institute for the Study of Drug Dependence): (0207) 9281211
Information centre for drugs.

Websites

You can find out lots more about drugs on the Internet. Many websites have been put together by young people. Other sites are run by organisations to provide information and advice. Some sites show pictures of different drugs and explain the effects.

Websites change all the time, but try these:

www.drugscope.co.uk
Run by the ISDD. May be useful if you do a drugs project. Click on their Links button for information on other websites.

www.trashed.co.uk
Run by the Health Promotion Service. Drugs news and information.

www.d-code.co.uk
A good drug education site.

www.hea.org.uk/locate
Another drug education site.

Glossary of words used about drugs

abuse	The wrong way of treating something or someone.
addict	Someone who cannot give something up.
addictive	Habit-forming, something you cannot give up.
AIDS	Illnesses that often develop from HIV infection.
alcoholic	Someone addicted to alcohol.
caution	A legal warning given for some offences.
controlled drugs	Drugs that are covered by certain laws.
courier	Someone who carries drugs for another person.
dependent	Needing something for support.
depressant	A drug that calms you down or makes you less active.
drug baron	A rich criminal who controls drug supplies.
hallucinate	To see or imagine things that are not real.
hallucinogenic	A drug that makes you see or imagine things.
hangover	A terrible feeling after drinking too much alcohol.

high	Feeling good on drugs.
HIV	A virus that attacks the body's immune system.
hooked	Addicted or dependent on something.
illegal	Against the law.
infection	An attack on the body by germs.
joint	Cigarette rolled with cannabis.
nicotine	An addictive drug found in tobacco.
prescribe	To write an order for drugs.
probation	Legal supervision instead of prison.
reefer	A cigarette rolled with cannabis.
rush	A sudden short 'high' that goes to the head.
sleeping pills	Medicine that helps you sleep.
spliff	A cigarette rolled with cannabis.
sterile	Free from germs.
steroids	Anabolic steroids, a kind of stimulant.
substance	A general term for different kinds of 'stuff'.
trafficking	Transporting drugs.
vapour	A fine mist or gas.
Youth Justice Service	A local court that deals with young offenders.

Index